Hannah Stone

The Invisible Worm

Indigo Dreams Publishing

First Edition: The Invisible Worm
First published in Great Britain in 2023 by:
Indigo Dreams Publishing
24, Forest Houses
Cookworthy Moor
Halwill
Beaworthy
Devon
EX21 5UU

www.indigodreamspublishing.com

Hannah Stone has asserted her right under the Copyright, Designs and Patents Act 1988 to be identified as the author of this work.
© Hannah Stone 2023

ISBN 978-1-912876-82-2

British Library Cataloguing in Publication Data. A CIP record for this book can be obtained from the British Library.

Designed and typeset in Palatino Linotype by Indigo Dreams.
Cover image by Oz Hardwick
Printed and bound in Great Britain by 4edge Ltd.

Papers used by Indigo Dreams are recyclable products made from wood grown in sustainable forests following the guidance of the Forest Stewardship Council.

In memoriam Rosemary Mitchell

(1967-2021)

Acknowledgements

A version of **Additional Death in a Time of Pandemic** was published in *Dreich: poems from the Earth* (2021).

Embarking was published in *Dreich 8* (2022).

Great Beauty and **Forget Me Not** were written in memory of Rosemary's parents and each poem was used in the order of service for their funerals.

Some of the **Tuscan Haiku** were published in *Coast to Coast to Coast* Issue 6, Summer 2019.

Evening Stroll from Gap Cottage was shortlisted in York Amnesty International competition on the theme of 'Locked' and published in their website May 2021, and also on the Poetry Wivenhoe website.

Life-Cycle: on My Late Mother's Charm Bracelet was originally published in *Holding up Half the Sky*, Rosemary Mitchell and Hannah Stone (Indigo Dreams Publishing, 2019).

I want to live ... was originally published in *Hopes and Joys, Astonishment and Tears*, Rosemary Mitchell, ed. Hannah Stone (Indigo Dreams Publishing, 2022).

CONTENTS

II A Testament of Friendship

The Invisible Worm

Preface

Rosemary Mitchell was a scholar, and Deacon in the Church of England. She was also my friend, and during the lockdowns of the Covid-19 Pandemic we were each other's 'support bubble.' In the spring of 2021 it became clear she was unwell, and within a very few months she had been diagnosed with an aggressive cancer, from which she died within weeks of her diagnosis. As a single woman, an only child, she had asked me (as her friend and former colleague) to act as her nominated next of kin and one of her executors; little did we know at the time this would involve engaging in end of life care. These poems record that experience – and the joyful times we shared in earlier years on holidays together in the north of England, Malta, and Italy.

Until a year or so before her death, Rosemary was engaged in an academic career, as a Professor of History at Leeds Trinity University, where I had worked as a colleague. She was the most generous and community-minded of people and when the then Department of English, under the directorship of Oz Hardwick, established a Creative Writing Programme, she responded enthusiastically to the opportunity to get involved. We needed a 'brand' name for the Open Mic event that was being set up, and it was Rosemary's suggestion of 'Wordspace' that emerged as the front runner. I then appropriated the concept and devised a logo for it, suggesting in one of my MA (Creative Writing) exercises that this become an imprint for writing associated with Leeds Trinity University. This grandiose suggestion was carefully shaped by Oz into an enduring relationship with Indigo Dreams Publishing, who published my collaboration with fellow MA students Gill Lambert and Maria Stevenson, *An After Dinner's Sleep*, in 2015, and a collaboration with Rosemary, *Holding up Half the Sky* (2019). IDP also generously agreed to publish a privately circulated, posthumous, edition of Rosemary's own poems, *Hopes and Joys, Astonishment and Tears*, edited by me in 2022. It is therefore the most enormous pleasure that this current volume is a Wordspace publication, and I offer most sincere thanks to Oz Hardwick for his innumerable and unstinting contributions to the literary life of Leeds Trinity University.

Many thanks also to Ronnie and Dawn for all they do in supporting the publication of poetry. Thanks are also due to Clare Wigzell for reading first drafts and for all her encouragement. I would also like to thank and honour Joyce, Amina, Jane, Margaret, Heather and Di who shared and supported so generously those final days of Rosemary's life. Thanks are also due to Tom Lusty and Helen Reid, whose home in Kettlewell provided a tranquil refuge for editing these poems.

I

The Invisible Worm

'O Rose, thou are sick…'

(William Blake)

Un-Magnificat

Who would have thought your maiden womb
could conceive such horrors?
Your 'yes' to God's call deafened you
to that other annunciation;
you stopped your ears to the healing need
of the woman with a haemorrhage,
and chose to Martha your mother.
How she will scold you, now
you are together again,
in a place where you can both be Marys,
sitting at the feet of your Lord.

Short-changed

Behold, I tell you a mystery; we shall not all sleep, but we shall all be changed; in a moment, in the twinkling of an eye, at the last trumpet. (I Cor. 15: 51-2)

You blamed 'the change' for the bulges
which gestated inside you;
insatiable twins dancing on your bladder,
purloining your breath, extorting
bigger clothes, while begrudging room
for even one slice of cake.

You are advised to take no valuables
onto the ward, so hand me your purse,
for safekeeping. I spend the small change
of your final trimester on fruit and nuts,
books, and tempting beverages,
to distract you from the usury
of ward-round updates.

With each stolen night of rest, you shrink
inside the hospital gown, which strains
to contain the tumours
which have embezzled your life.

The Guard Dog of Ward 96

Cerberus, in sterile rubber gloves,
presses the buzzer
to release the catch; snaps
at the heels of visitors permitted
temporary admission from the place of plague,
forces them to make their mark
in the register of the pure.
Cerberus, in blue-belted tunic,
keeps her finger on the pulse.
Doles out jujubes of forgetfulness
in frilly paper cups;
chants words of doom inside the mask.
Behind her back, some souls, intrepid, dare
to sidle underneath the bolted door.

Additional Death in a Time of Pandemic

Apotropaic symbols sketched
on the locked door of oncology
are erased by swipes of sanitiser.

Posies of healing herbs bound
with a scrap of ribbon are left
on the window sill,

but they cannot evict your succubus,
and all the offered spells bleed out,
pale and drained

from working double-shifts,
protecting the nation
from Covid-19.

Diagnosis, Minus Three Weeks

'It's mischievous,' is all the doctor can say, 'the more aggressive because you're younger.' Sarcoma masquerading as a Puckish sprite, playfully lobbing a bomb into your womb, setting the timer, and running away. Its red flags left to flap in the breeze. Sarcoma lodged 'like a champagne cork' in your pelvis, where it dams the tributaries from vital organs; an impish landslide forcing the re-routing of veins, the routing of stents to keep things flowing. When your swelling belly played knock-down-ginger years ago, your clever brain said you were out. Now, we tilt-touch tips of plastic cups of Appletize, in mimicry of glasses of Prosecco, shared on holidays. We're having a ball on Gyne-Oncology, pass the wait for the ward-round with a go at 'who wrote me' – a game which you'll always win.

White

Wan cheeks replace rosy glow.
Bleached sheets wrap wasted limbs.
Blanched pillows propping your hideous gestation.

In the untenanted house, your worn-once alb droops
like a hopeless ghost,
shouldering unused day clothes in the cupboard,

and blank pages flutter in the diary
as plans erase themselves.

There is white noise in the ether, where words
blench and stagger beneath their weight.

Labore est Orare

(to pray is to work)

Friends promise consolation,
grafting hard at petitions
for your recovery.

I read up on Faust,
broker bargain-basement deals
with your impatient God,

but the contracts
are not honoured,
and prayer has gone on strike.

Hold Tight
And, underneath, the ever-lasting arms (Deut. 33:27).

Some days, you seem already
to have left us, gone
to join adoring parents,
hand-in-hand with trust.

Wanting occupation, I open
and close drawers; trot up
and down the stairs with armfuls of clothes,
folded for the charity shop.

When I enter the ward
you are wheeled out,
a brave smile pinned
above the hospital gown,

because today, your hand extracts
from mine the promise
to hold tight, when the time comes
for you to let you go.

Embarking
(ref Tennyson, 'Crossing the Bar')

You trust to see
your pilot
face to face

here on the shore
friends cling
to the rope

which tethers us,
pay it out
a yard at a time,

anticipating the friction burn
as its final thread snaps
and slips from our grasp.

This Room

...in the house still barely
a twinkle-in-the-eye of home,
was where tea was poured

into rosy, porcelain cups,
and laugher flowed,
as cake-crumbs were licked from sticky thumbs.

This was the room where your death
was birthed, women with bowels
of compassion breathing through your pains,

dry-eyed death doulas, crying inside,
wrapping their fingers round your hands
as they grow still, and, finally, chill.

Inventing New Gods

('As flies to wanton boys are we to th' gods;
They kill us for their sport'
~ *King Lear*, Act 4, Sc 1.)

There does not need to be pain,
they promise, tapping the syringe-driver,
indicating the 'gold-line' telephone number.
So, can we call on Midas
in those liminal hours? He could insinuate
himself into the room whose sofa
made way for hospital bed,
the room where we take turns to watch with you,
our un-drugged sleep peopled with plot-less dreams.

Beneath the window, a bodkin is stalled
in an unfinished tapestry –
half a rose, a green stem, the spine
of a leaf – dozing, you remember Beth
laying aside the needle which had become
'too heavy'; the mice in Gloucester shouting
'no more twist!' You jerk awake,
and realise it was not Thanatos
but Atropos hammering at the door,
and there, on the threshold,
blocking the first glimmer of dawn,
stands the palliative care nurse,
holding aloft the frayed ends
of your amputated life.

Vigil

There was agony,
yes, but not Gethsemane:
you were not alone.

Religio
(def: 'obligation, the bond between (hu)man and the gods')
Genesis 22

I marvel at Abraham's faith
that the Almighty would loosen the bonds
which tied his son
to the sacrificial slab,
releasing as proxy for the beloved heir
a ram, trapped in the thicket.

I do not share your belief
in a god who cheats death
out of your soul by sending
his only child to die on a cross.
Even that man-god wept
when his own friend died.

We are bound by love, though you
are released from life's shackles,
and so I flood these pages
with words; shed tears enough to
overflow a lacrymarium
for which I have no votive shrine.

Seeds of Faith

My credulity does not stretch
to share your expectation
of the afterlife as a continuum
of what we shared on earth.

Across the path to your empty house
strawberry plants shoot out suckers,
linking with tentative latticework
straggly lawn and overgrown hedge.

'Leave the dead seed-heads',
you instruct the gardener, finding
their 'structure' pleasing; too much neatness
did not suit you.

I'm blind as Thomas, but suspect you'll see
your risen Lord, configured as the gardener,
garnering souls beyond the empty tomb,
and sowing seeds of faith.

Somewhere

Rainbows do heavy lifting.
They yoke together the full spectrum
of dark shades and bright tones,
span temporary bridges between
scattered communities,
bind jaded adults to the confidence
of infant innocence.
Travelling home from your funeral,
friends note a rainbow, cheering
the Leeds skyline. They share it on Facebook,
remembering how you could always find,
amidst the shit, a crock of gold.

A Valediction, Proscribing Mourning

Your friends tell me I must make space
to grieve, and offer up the jagged bits
of their distress, for my release.

This jigsaw of pain and loss fails
to reframe the image of your death;
those voices cannot pierce
the numbness in me, now
your voice has gone.

Don't get me wrong, there were occasions
when I craved silence in your company,
wanted to watch a film
or stand in front of a painting
without your annotations,
and recitation of captions;
times I would have settled
for in-the-moment blissful ignorance,
my mossy imagination packing the gaps
between the stones of information –
but you needed to share your knowledge.

Visiting the Tate, I witness Turners;
and, as I stroll from one gallery to the next,
I slip back into your sitting room,
and hear again the clamour
of your interjection above the actors' dialogue,
giving chapter and verse of the romance
between the painter and Sophia Booth
(which I had just intuited).

I would give good money now
for the sketch of your life to be completed,
to achieve more than these bold blobs
of colour shouting 'fire' through the mist,
for your boat to be sailing
into the blaze of a new dawn,
not scuppered, scuttled, wrecked.

Here, in this gallery,
I find a place to mourn,
for you have passed into another room,
my tears are dammed,
and you are dumb.

In Heaven

there must be bluebell woods, you insisted,
or you'll want to know the reason why,
when we walked together, there, last May.

In Rougement Woods
I wade through seas of fragrance,
binding memories of you close
like a jiggling baby in a sling,
heart-beat and steps in sync.

Laved by overnight rain
the woods dissolve into birdsong,
explode in drifts of blue and white
where ransoms lace the river bank.

On the shore, where pairs of swans
sample the peace, I ask
'Is it as you commanded?'
but there is no reply, save the robins' flutey duet,
and the blackbird obbligato.

They are singing from a different score to me
and I do not know the words.

21 June, 2022, Hay on Wye
(For Joyce)

Never did so small a bird sing with so loud a voice,
as this cocky wren, shouting down the Mistle Thrush,
contradicting the ducks that skim the river.
Beyond the bridge, the water breaks and remakes
itself round islands, small plots of land
that dream of more than waterfowl and willows.
Today, we, too, shall be broken and remade,
as we gather to scatter your ashes; your death
the boulder in the living flow,
forcing us to find new currents.
This woodland, riverside, walk is blessed
with birdsong, and every green smell of a June morning,
where water, air and light perform their diurnal task of beauty,
an icon *Acheiropoieta* – not made with hands –
and, in restoring you to the earth,
we write anew that promise to be held in love's embrace.

II
A Testament of Friendship

Great Beauty
(i.m. Leslie Mitchell, 2014)

A Great Beauty visited him
as he rocked between life and death,
shuffling in clean sheets to find
the next resting place.
And she came in the kindness of carers,
was found in family love;
and great beauty was in your sweet temper,
your passion to communicate
with those you never saw,
in your stubbornness and dottiness.
And now a Great Beauty greets you,
setting aside the broken body of her son,
who she rocked, oh so gently, on her knee.

Forget Me Not
(i.m. Eileen Philippa Mitchell, 2017)

She didn't need to say it,
though her Celtic eyes were passionate
with messages, fierce at times.
You'll always remember the woman she was
before age stole her energy,
before infirmity ransacked her dexterity.
And you'll never forget being buoyed up
by the love you gave each other.
Such love is not lost in grief;
it merely seeks a new home.
Lie on the lawn, and count the shades of blue;
Forget me nots trespassing beneath the fence,
bluebells attentive under apple blossom,
and that spring sky which reminds you
French has no other word for heaven
but the one which speaks of this sun-infused hue.
When your sky is washed with rain
(which the French call tears)
and there's only enough blue
to make a pair of sailor's trousers,
take it, drape it around your shoulders.
It will stretch. It will suffice.

A Testament of Friendship

I

Valetta, Malta

Other echoes
Inhabit the garden. Shall we follow?
(Burnt Norton)

In a hot climate, new companions
share more than the leaven
of conversation.
You master the air con, while I
restock a plate with chunks of water melon,
chilled from the fridge.
Filched figs burst their sweetness
in our mouths,
skins warmed by evening sunlight.
We queue for local buses, board ferries
to visit ancient worlds.
Take tickets for the trips
into each other's pasts.

II

Rudston, East Yorkshire

Home is where one starts from. As we grow older
The world becomes strange, the pattern more complicated
Of dead and living.
(East Coker)

'She has come home, bringing her laurels with her,'
 a villager said, when the wold child returned
in a coffin flanked by a profligacy of southern lilies.
She'd prayed for life enough to do her work;
loved – jealously – rewrote histories
in stuffy rooms far from the fold.
Decades later, readers come
to trace her epitaph on lichened stone;
watch the long shadow
of the red stone count but one decade
of her life for each of its millennia,
friends bringing together verso and recto
of the books they share,
stretched on sofas after a day of sightseeing.

III

Northumberland

The sea has many voices,
Many gods and many voices.
(Dry Salvages)

This sea has many moods
and innumerable small bays,
but this one promised privacy
for your swim in the briny.
It was somewhere near a helicopter station,
I repeated, peering
at the splayed fractals on the OS map
as we turned from the coast road to the dunes.
The weather colluded with your modesty,
draping Howdiemont sands in sudden harr.
A short dip sufficed;
these northern shores yield little warmth.
Burnished by salt water, your rosy face
beams its smiles
above the swaddling towels.

IV

Firenze

And what the dead had no speech for
They can tell you, being dead. When living, the communication
Of the dead is tongued with fire, beyond the language of the living.
(Little Gidding)

And so, the Spirit descends.
Whether we are ready or not
to hand them over into safekeeping.

And thus we shall learn grief is love annealed;
as bodies cool, their passions remain tempered by tears;
do not quench them, for in their flowing lies your strength.

So put on the armour of fellowship;
gird yourself with friends to laugh with.
We walk new paths and find fresh delights.

And in an Italian dawn, when you wake and weep,
reach for my hand as we listen
to the nightingale's gift of rapture.

We think of Keats, in his Roman sarcophagus;
a short man, a short life, but every year
of every life rings true when love strikes its bell.

Tuscan Haiku

Italian opera
provides the vocabulary:
'Io son felice'

luscious olive oil,
smoky, peppery and green,
soaks into bread chunks

audacious waiter
does pull-ups on the doorframe
to the terrazzo

Boboli gardens
turning into a dustbowl;
fountains not working

beggars on pavements
prostrated as if in prayer
ask for our small change

San Gimignano
suffered much from the Black Death,
and now from tourism

Saint Sebastian
holds out his cloak to protect
citizens from plague

grapes have attitude
as big as small English plums
bursting with flavour

beggars at red lights
contemporary mendicants
hold up plastic bowls

'Holy Trinity
undergoing maintenance.'
I have days like that

pilgrims now follow
the Via Francigena
using Googlemaps

a small olive grove
punctuated by cypress;
fresco or for real?

dragons and demons
tend to populate frescos
more than other beasts

Moses' transformed staff
looks more dragon than serpent,
though how would I know?

St. Fina's plank bed
stands upright in the chapel;
she, too, was raised up.

a small signora
flaps her duster at tourists;
shutters out the day.

Evening Stroll from Gap Cottage
(Hadrian's Wall)

An evening stroll, the first for months, with friend.
Unlocked from Covid's jail, new freedoms found:
A map to hand, a path ahead, our end

Not fixed. Relaxed, our ears take in the sound
Of tractors baling hay, and twitt'ring birds
Above us, or arising from the ground –

Familiar sounds, but now as if unheard
Before today's permission to return
To fellowship, to sharing; we are stirred

By this 'new normal'; a glad license earned
By months of solitude (confinement, too).
Observing protocol, our bodies yearned

For touch, or scent; subliminal small clues
Humanity was wont, before the screen,
To use as anchors while our knowledge grew

Advancing from the infant's primal scream
To adult expectations of a life
Oft shared with others, purposeful; a means

To craft communities, devoid of strife
When sharing time. Just being in a room
With others, talking, fostered the belief

That such communication was a boon
To bond society, engender peace.
Now boomers become generation zoom

Our discourse virtual, and with this decrease
In visceral contact we are cast adrift
On choppy seas. Anxieties increase

In absence of proximity, that gift
Few took for granted, when available.
Now, walking close enough to chat, we sift

Through thoughts, share memories; the air is full
Of words, the sounds of farmers harvesting
Long grass that swishes past our legs. The wall

We follow holds its histories, beck'ning
Each generation since to empathise
With Roman soldiers, the occupying

Army Hadrian sent to colonise,
Extend his empire; ossify the rule
He instigated for communities

That showed the values he laid down for all
Who craved the status 'citizen of Rome.'
We walked for several hours, beneath the jewel

Of evening sun, and then began to roam
Towards the house which was, for three days, home.

Notes

Epigrams in **A Testament of Friendship** are from T.S. Eliot's Four Quartets.

The title **A Testament of Friendship** refers to the book by Vera Brittain about her friendship with Winifred Holtby, who was born in Rudston and, after a life spent in the metropolis, was buried there.

Envoi

For further reading of my work, on a much wider range of themes, see the following, which may be purchased, where appropriate, from Indigo Dreams Publishing directly or by contacting me on hannahstone14@hotmail.com. I am also available for poetry readings, workshops, and broadcasts.

New Crops from Old Fields: Eight Medievalist Poets (Ed. Oz Hardwick, Stairwell Books, 2015)
An After-Dinner's Sleep (with Gill Lambert and Maria Preston, Indigo Dreams Publishing, 2015)
Lodestone (Stairwell Books, 2016)
Missing Miles (Indigo Dreams Publishing, 2017)
Swn Y Morloi (Maytree Press, 2019)
Holding up Half the Sky (with Rosemary Mitchell, Indigo Dreams Publishing, 2019)
Fit to Bust (with Pamela Scobie, Runcible Spoon Press, 2020)
Reflections: A Poet-Theologian in Lockdown Leeds (Maytree Press, 2021)

Life-Cycle: on My Late Mother's Charm Bracelet by Rosemary Mitchell

It starts with a *Turtle*, ancient world-bearer
slow-rolling out your lifespan with a secret smile.
Destiny dictates, too, a *Spinning-Wheel*, where your humble
history's spun. No royal finger's pricked, though:
you're but a doctor's daughter, woven in Wales,
so here's a *Fleur-de-Lys*, a prince's feather for
your country, and a *Miner's Lamp* for your forbears.
Your grandfather struck black gold from a coal-face. And I recall
now that you hammered on a typewriter at the Coal Board
in the fifties. And here hangs a *Chimney-Sweep*, top-hatted
with his lucky ladder: a cheeky promise of fortune for a bride
on her wedding day. About the middle of the chain, a *Heart* is
fastened fast, close to a *Welsh Love-Spoon*, and a *Scout Hat*:
these three spell Dad! A green-tinted tiny china *Tyrolean Hat*
hanging nearby, recalls with a porcelain clarity your holidays.
Ever you loved a mountain – and a drink, the *Tankard* tells me.
And that *Leather Bottle*, did it once hold wine?
A *Silver Bird* swoops in, letter in beak: a message, perhaps
for the mother *Cow*? Sometime after I am born, the *Sled*
begins to slide downhill. But there's still *Leo*, your birth-sign:
you're brave of heart, and will rage against the dying of *Green Light*.
Towards the end, I see the signs of passing time, a blue-flowered *Bell*
and a *Clock*, which ticks to termination in a *Cathedral*'s Shade.
Your circle's closed; the charms are all told. I wrap
and lock your bracelet in a chest, imprison you as soundly as
I can in the *Round Tower* of my weeping heart.

I want to live .... by Rosemary Mitchell

I want to live because –
I haven't eaten pierogi
I haven't been to Sorrento
I haven't seen *Citizen Kane*
I haven't played Bezique
I haven't walked the Camino
I haven't sat on a jury
I haven't grown a tomato –
But most of all because
I haven't loved nearly enough.

Indigo Dreams Publishing Ltd
24, Forest Houses
Cookworthy Moor
Halwill
Beaworthy
Devon
EX21 5UU
www.indigodreamspublishing.com